Beyond Gerrymandering

How Wisconsin's New Legislative Maps Provide Hope for a More Representative Government

Freeman Trends

Table Of Contents

1: Introduction

History of Wisconsin Gerrymandering

Like many other states in the union, Wisconsin has a long history of gerrymandering—the deliberate redrawing of election district lines to give one political party the upper hand. Elbridge Gerry, the governor of Massachusetts in 1812, created an extremely asymmetrical electoral district that was compared to a salamander, which is where the term "gerrymander" originated. Over time, Wisconsin's experience with gerrymandering has changed to reflect changes in political power and judicial challenges.

The Development of Wisconsin Gerrymandering

Since the early years of statehood, gerrymandering has influenced Wisconsin's political environment. But Wisconsin's recent gerrymandering history begins in the early 2010s when Republicans took over the state legislature and the governorship. Republicans were able to alter legislative districts after the 2010 census, a procedure that greatly benefited their party, thanks to this consolidation of power.

State Legislative Maps' Importance

The process of creating state legislative maps is very important because it establishes the borders of electoral districts, which affects how political power is distributed. All citizens' votes are given equal weight, and communities are suitably represented in the legislative process, thanks to fair and representative maps. Gerrymandered maps, on the other hand, undermine democratic values and result in disproportionate representation by undermining the integrity of the voting process. Legislative map manipulation has been a divisive topic in Wisconsin, as the ruling party uses redistricting to uphold its political hegemony. Politicians can easily entrench their authority and hinder competitive elections by carefully dividing up districts to concentrate opposition voters while distributing their supporters among safe seats.

A Synopsis of the New Law Maps

In Wisconsin, the adoption of new legislative maps has been the focus of much discussion and legal examination. Republicans controlled the state legislature, which was tasked with redrawing electoral boundaries after the 2020 census. Critics contend that by promoting Republican interests and reducing the voting strength of places leaning Democratic, the resulting maps uphold gerrymandering.

The newly constructed legislative maps are blatant examples of partisanship at work, with districts created to maximize Republican representation and minimize Democratic chances of winning elections. This tactic, called "packing and cracking," entails dispersing supporters throughout several districts to lessen their influence while concentrating opposing votes into a small number of districts to restrict their influence.

Importance of the Governor's Decision

The governor plays a vital role in the redistricting process because they have the power to veto or adopt the proposed maps. The Republican-drawn maps were vetoed by Democratic Governor Tony Evers of Wisconsin because of concerns about their constitutionality and fairness. Evers' veto highlights the wider partisan split over redistricting and serves as a major check on the authority of the Republican-controlled legislature.

The governor's move also emphasizes how crucial executive supervision is to guarantee that redistricting is carried out in a way that preserves democratic values and safeguards the rights of every individual. In addition to demonstrating his readiness to confront partisan excess, Governor Evers reinforces his commitment to fairness and transparency in the electoral process by rejecting gerrymandered maps.

In Wisconsin, gerrymandering is still a divisive topic that has significant effects on democratic governance and electoral justice. The public's confidence in the political system is damaged by the manipulation of legislative maps, which goes against the idea of one person, one vote. The governor and other important players' decisions throughout the ongoing redistricting dispute will have a lasting impact on Wisconsin's democracy and beyond.

2: Historical Context of Republican Dominance

Wisconsin is a microcosm of the electoral dynamics across the country, right at the center of American politics. The story of power struggles, electoral complexities, and legal challenges in the Badger State is captivating, ranging from the GOP's firm hold on state politics to the divisive debates over legislative redistricting. This paper explores three major subtopics influencing Wisconsin politics: GOP Domination in Wisconsin Politics, Gerrymandering's Effect on Election Results, and Issues with Earlier Legislative Maps.

Republican Domination in Wisconsin Politics

The Republican Party has recently had a significant influence on Wisconsin politics. The majority of congressional seats, the governorship, and the state legislature have all been controlled by the GOP since the early 2010s. Because of their majority, Republicans have been able to enact several legislative goals that have shaped the state's socioeconomic structure, from labor reforms to tax cuts.

The Republican tsunami that swept the nation in the 2010 midterm elections is what laid the foundation for GOP rule in Wisconsin. Republican successes at the state and federal levels were noteworthy in Wisconsin, where they were driven by the grassroots conservative movement and the general dissatisfaction with the Obama administration. With his election as governor, Scott Walker ushered in a period of Republican rule that was defined by audacious policy proposals and intense political division.

Wisconsin's congressional delegation reflects the Republican majority in the state's politics.

Wisconsin's congressional map has been crafted to benefit Republicans despite the state being a battleground in presidential elections, in part because of the practice of gerrymandering. Even in years when statewide elections are hotly contested, the GOP has been able to hold onto a majority of congressional seats thanks to careful redistricting.

Effect of Gerrymandering on Results of Elections

The process of redrawing electoral district lines to give one political party the advantage over another, known as gerrymandering, has had a major impact on Wisconsin's election results. Every ten years, after the U.S. Census, redistricting takes place, giving the ruling party a chance to reconfigure legislative boundaries in a way that strengthens its advantage in politics.

Following the 2010 Census, Wisconsin's Republican-controlled legislature used the redistricting process to redraw legislative borders in a way that greatly benefited their party. Republicans essentially assured their control in the state legislature for years to come by clustering Democratic supporters into a small number of districts and distributing Republican votes throughout a larger number of districts.

Gerrymandering affects not just state legislature elections but also congressional elections in terms of electoral outcomes. Republicans drew Wisconsin's congressional map following the 2010 Census, and it has garnered criticism for being unbalanced and lacking in competition. Because of this, even though Wisconsin is known for being a politically competitive state, the state's congressional delegation has remained largely Republican.

Problems with the Legislative Maps of the Past

Notwithstanding the Republican Party's enduring influence in Wisconsin politics, objections to the validity of legislative maps have surfaced recently. Gerrymandering's detractors contend that by limiting some groups' ability to vote and solidifying the positions of political incumbents, the practice subverts the fundamentals of democracy.

The most well-known legal challenge to Wisconsin's legislative maps was Gill v. Whitford, a historic case that made it to the U.S. Supreme Court in 2017. A group of Democratic voters filed the lawsuit, claiming that Republican-favored legislative maps in Wisconsin were unconstitutionally gerrymandered, robbing Democratic voters of their right to representation.

Even though the Supreme Court avoided discussing partisan gerrymandering in its decision, the case raised awareness of the problem nationwide and spurred new attempts to alter Wisconsin's and other states' redistricting procedures. Some states have implemented independent redistricting commissions or other initiatives to lessen the impact of partisan politics on the redistricting process in response to public demand and legal challenges.

Advocacy groups and political activists in Wisconsin are continuing their attempts to question the validity of legislative maps to achieve more equitable and open redistricting practices. The continuous discussion surrounding gerrymandering emphasizes how crucial it is to make sure that electoral districts are created in a way that respects democratic values and represents the will of the electorate, even though the results of these attempts are yet unknown.

Gerrymandering, challenges to prior legislative maps, and GOP control all interact to determine Wisconsin's political landscape. The Republican Party's hegemony in state politics and the effects of gerrymandering on election results underscore the intricate dynamics involved in the political process. The fight for just and representative democracy is still going strong as Wisconsin struggles to overcome these obstacles.

3: Legal and Political Battles

Suits Regarding Districts That Were Gerrymandered

In democratic nations, the practice of redrawing election district lines to give preference to one political party or group over another is known as gerrymandering. As a result, legal action against gerrymandered districts has gained popularity among individuals looking to address alleged irregularities in the voting process.

The Equal Protection Clause of the Fourteenth Amendment to the United States Constitution, which upholds the idea of "one person, one vote," is frequently at the center of these legal disputes. According to this idea, every person, regardless of where they live, should have about the same amount of voting power as every other person. Gerrymandering can be viewed as a breach of this fundamental protection when it skews district borders to reduce the voting power of particular groups.

Gill v. Whitford (2018) is a noteworthy case from recent years that contested Wisconsin's partisan gerrymandering laws. The plaintiffs contended that Democratic voters had been deprived of their constitutional rights because the Republican-controlled legislature had altered electoral districts unconstitutionally to benefit their party. In the end, the case made its way to the US Supreme Court, which decided that the plaintiffs lacked standing to file the complaint even if it did not rule on the case's merits. Nonetheless, the Court left the matter unresolved at the federal level and did not completely shut the door on political gerrymandering lawsuits in the future.

State-level litigation challenging gerrymandered districts is common, in addition to federal challenges. Legal objections to gerrymandering can be based on the provisions of state constitutions and statutes that provide fair and equitable representation. For instance, the Pennsylvania Supreme Court declared in 2018 that the state's congressional map was unconstitutionally biased toward Republicans and invalidated it. Redrawing the map in a fair and unbiased way was mandated by the court, which resulted in a more equitable distribution of electoral districts.

The success of legal actions against gerrymandered districts might differ according to the jurisdiction and particulars of each case, even despite legal challenges. The fact that some lawsuits have been successful in forcing changes and eradicating gerrymandered maps while others have been rejected or dismissed by judges highlights the difficulty of the legal landscape surrounding electoral redistricting.

Legal precedents and judicial rulings

Future redistricting attempts and the terrain of gerrymandering litigation are significantly shaped by judicial decisions and legal precedents. Court rulings on partisan gerrymandering's constitutional ramifications have the potential to set significant legal precedents and regulations that control the redistricting process.

The United States Supreme Court first addressed the problem of political gerrymandering in Davis v. Bandemer (1986), a seminal case that has had a tremendous influence on the legal framework around gerrymandering. Though the Court held that partisan gerrymandering that is too excessive could potentially violate the Equal Protection Clause of the Fourteenth Amendment, it established a difficult standard of proof for establishing such claims, requiring plaintiffs to show that their actions have both discriminatory intent and impact. This decision set a precedent that influenced the burden of proof and the standards used by judges in political gerrymandering litigation that followed.

The Supreme Court examined whether allegations of partisan gerrymandering were justiciable, or appropriate for judicial settlement, in the crucial 2004 decision of Vieth v. Jubelirer. Despite the Court's extreme division on the matter and the lack of a majority ruling, the case highlighted the difficulties in developing a judicially workable criterion for assessing allegations of partisan gerrymandering. Despite this loss, the Court urged more research into alternate methods for determining whether or not gerrymandered districts are lawful, and it left open the potential for future advances in the law.

In cases like Department of Commerce v. New York (2019) and Rucho v. Common Cause (2019), the Supreme Court has recently heard arguments regarding partisan gerrymandering once more. The Court decided in Rucho that allegations of partisan gerrymandering raise political issues that are outside the purview of federal courts, thereby blocking federal judicial remedies for resolving the matter. With this ruling, the Court's stance on partisan gerrymandering underwent a dramatic change, reducing the judiciary's ability to monitor voting district borders.

Notwithstanding these defeats, court decisions and established legal precedents persist in defining the parameters of gerrymandering cases and providing direction to plaintiffs, legislators, and subordinate courts. Even if there is still uncertainty around the Supreme Court's partisan gerrymandering doctrine, continuing legal developments present chances for advocacy, change, and the pursuit of electoral justice.

Public Attitude and Political Influence

The discourse around gerrymandering is greatly influenced by public opinion and political pressure, as are initiatives to remedy the problem through grassroots activity and legislative measures.

A fundamental concern of the public is the fairness and equity of the voting process. Voters lose faith in the democratic process and their elected representatives when they believe that electoral district lines have been changed to benefit one party over another. Because of this, policies aimed at preventing gerrymandering and advancing impartiality and transparency in redistricting frequently have broad public support.

There are several ways that public opinion can be expressed, such as voter initiatives, advocacy campaigns, and neighborhood organizing projects. In certain places, like Michigan and Colorado, for instance, voters have taken matters into their own hands by approving ballot initiatives to create impartial redistricting commissions entrusted with creating election maps devoid of political bias. A growing desire among voters to take back control of the redistricting process and make sure that electoral districts are formed in a way that represents the interests of the larger community is reflected in these grassroots campaigns.

Political pressure, along with grassroots movement, is a major factor in determining how states and the federal government respond to gerrymandering. Intense disputes over redistricting frequently occur between political parties, interest groups, and elected officials as they try to obtain a tactical edge in upcoming elections. Redistricting decisions are influenced by partisanship, incumbency protection, and demographic changes, which can result in heated discussions and party impasse.

Nonetheless, the public's scrutiny and the media's attention can put pressure on legislators to make accountability and fairness the top priorities during the redistricting process. Prominent instances of gerrymandering, such as those that make national news or provoke strong public opinion, have the power to mobilize support for reform initiatives and force elected authorities to act. Furthermore, the possibility of negative electoral outcomes or legal challenges might act as a disincentive for extreme cases of partisan gerrymandering, encouraging legislators to be more cautious when creating electoral maps.

Growing public awareness of gerrymandering in recent years has given reform movements nationwide impetus. The goal of fighting gerrymandering is to ensure that every voter's voice is heard and to protect democratic principles through grassroots mobilization and legislative campaigning.

Political pressure and public opinion, judicial decisions and precedents, lawsuits against gerrymandered districts, and public opinion all play a part in how electoral redistricting is shaped. Even if gerrymandering is still a problem in democratic countries, efforts to solve it show a dedication to maintaining the fairness of elections and defending the fundamentals of representative democracy.

4: Governor's Decision and Its Implications

Few procedures in the intricate world of politics have as much influence over the democratic process as redistricting. The redistricting process is a crucial phase in the electoral cycle that affects everything from drawing electoral borders to defining the very limits of political power. The governor is at the center of this process, and decisions made by him or her could have a big impact. This paper investigates the governor's power throughout the redistricting process, considers the ramifications of their choice to approve new maps, looks at how it might affect the next elections, and looks at the reactions from advocacy organizations and political parties.

The Governor's Power in the Redistricting Procedure

Depending on the jurisdiction, the governor may have varying powers throughout the redistricting process. The governor is a key player in some states; he or she may veto proposed maps or take part in the redistricting commission directly. In others, the governor's power might be more circumstantial and restricted to accepting or rejecting legislatively issued maps.

Governors frequently wield considerable influence by their public remarks, political connections, and behind-the-scenes talks, regardless of the scope of their formal authority. Their choices have the power to reshape district boundaries, impacting community representation and the partisan balance.

Additionally, governors act as a check on gerrymandering, which is the practice of unjustly drafting district lines to benefit one political party over another. Governors can reduce the likelihood of gerrymandered maps that threaten democracy by advocating for justice, openness, and compliance with the law.

Evaluation of the Governor's Choice to Sign the New Maps

Governors must examine several variables when deciding whether to sign new maps, including prospective legal challenges, partisan interests, public opinion, and legal considerations. Their choice makes a strong statement about their adherence to the rule of law, justice, and democratic ideals.

When evaluating a governor's decision to sign new maps, considerations like how it will affect minority representation, electoral competitiveness, and constitutional values like population equality and contiguity are frequently taken into account. In addition, since the media, advocacy organizations, and voters have the power to influence the political climate in the run-up to elections, governors might take this into account.

Furthermore, the governor's decision's timeliness can be very important, particularly in states where judicial review of redistricting occurs or when deadlines are tight. A postponed decision can breed ambiguity, which makes it more difficult for candidates to run successful campaigns and for voters to make wise decisions.

Possible Effect on Upcoming Elections

The governor's decision to approve new maps has far-reaching effects that stretch well beyond the present political cycle. Redistricting affects the representation of various populations, the composition of congressional delegations, and the balance of power in legislatures, all of which have long-term effects on the political landscape.

The competitiveness of races, the capacity of disenfranchised groups to elect candidates of their choice, and the general legitimacy of the electoral process can all be significantly impacted, with potentially significant implications for future elections. The governor's choice may occasionally strengthen or undermine a specific party's hegemony, changing the nature of both state and federal politics.

District borders that are in line with political trends, urban-rural splits, and demographic changes may also have long-term effects on election results. While governors who put partisan advantage ahead of justice and inclusivity run the risk of undermining public confidence and escalating division, the former may promote a livelier and more representative democracy.

Political Parties and Advocacy Groups' Reaction

Given the significant stakes, political parties and advocacy organizations frequently respond angrily when the governor signs new maps. Depending on how the new maps impact their chances of winning elections, partisan organizations may celebrate the decision as a win for their cause or denounce it as a violation of democratic principles.

Civil rights, electoral reform, and good governance advocacy groups keep a close eye on the redistricting process and rally support from the public to demand equitable and transparent results. They could commend governors who put the needs of the people, fair standards, and objective evaluations first while denouncing those who give in to political pressure or backroom agreements.

Legal challenges to recently adopted maps are not unusual, especially where gerrymandering or voting rights abuses are suspected. The legitimacy and fairness of the redistricting process may be questioned, so governors need to be ready to defend their choices in court.

The governor has considerable influence over the redistricting process, which affects how elections are conducted, who makes up legislative bodies, and the very foundation of democracy. Their choices are closely watched and may have a significant impact on how various populations are represented in future elections. Governors must handle the difficulties of redistricting with honesty, openness, and a dedication to the values of equity and inclusivity in their capacity as custodians of the public trust.

5: Changes in Electoral Dynamics

capacity balance changes in political environments can completely change the course of legislation, the dynamics of minority representation, and the course of future political events. The power dynamics that support a country's or society's governance institutions change as those countries or societies do. Comprehending these changes and their possible consequences is essential for maneuvering through the intricate landscape of modern politics.

Recognizing Changes in the Balance of Power

A fundamental component of any examination of changes in political power is comprehending the forces behind these transitions. These can include social movements, geopolitical realignments, and changes in the economy and population. Globalization has been a major factor in recent years, connecting economies and countries in previously unheard-of ways. Technological developments have simultaneously given people and organizations more power and influence.

Furthermore, changes in the distribution of power frequently mirror broader changes in society, such as evolving perspectives on identity politics, governance, and the function of institutions. Power dynamics are always changing, reflecting how political systems are ever-changing, whether through democratic elections, popular upheavals, or institutional reforms.

Possible Impacts on the Legislative Schedule

Legislative agendas are affected by changes in the balance of power, which is one of the most obvious effects. As political parties or factions gain power, they frequently try to put their policies into reality, changing the legislative landscape in the process. Significant policy changes may arise from this, affecting everything from environmental laws and foreign policy endeavors to social welfare programs and economic improvements.

However, there are several variables, including the institutional structure, coalition dynamics, and public opinion, that affect how much of these changes happen. Power transfers in systems with checks and balances can result in compromise or deadlock, which slows the adoption of drastic measures. On the other hand, under more centralized systems, dominant parties or leaders might have more control over the legislative process and be able to pass their agenda with little resistance.

Significance for the Representation of Minorities

Changes in the distribution of power can have a significant impact on the representation of minorities in political institutions. Depending on the existing political dynamics, minorities—whether characterized by ethnicity, religion, philosophy, or other characteristics—often find themselves either sidelined or powerful. By amplifying minority voices, inclusive governance frameworks help guarantee that their issues are taken into consideration during legislative discussions.

Conversely, minorities may experience more marginalization, discrimination, or exclusion if power is concentrated in the hands of a dominant group. The ideals of democratic representation may be compromised by gerrymandering, restricted legislation, or election manipulation. Changes in power may also intensify already-existing tensions between majority and minority groups, sparking instability or violence in society.

Predicting Upcoming Political Situations

It takes a sophisticated understanding of historical patterns, contemporary dynamics, and new issues to predict future political situations. Although there is always some degree of uncertainty in forecasting, scenario planning can assist in identifying possible paths as well as the dangers and possibilities that come with them. Through the examination of diverse elements including population patterns, financial metrics, and international events, specialists can create several scenarios that assist in making strategic choices.

For instance, if populist groups keep gaining traction, the political environment might become more polarized, which would increase social divisions and policy instability. On the other hand, initiatives to address global issues like economic injustice and climate change can gather momentum in a world marked by inclusive government and multilateral collaboration, resulting in increased stability and prosperity.

Furthermore, technological developments like biotechnology and artificial intelligence are probably going to change the political environment in unexpected ways, bringing with them both opportunities and hazards. Data privacy, cybersecurity, and ethical governance are going to be major issues that influence public opinion and governmental agendas. Furthermore, changing demographics—such as aging populations and migration trends—will affect electoral dynamics and policy goals, requiring policymakers to adjust how they do business.

Changes in the balance of power have a significant impact on future political scenarios, minority representation, and legislative agendas. Policymakers and stakeholders can more effectively negotiate the complicated terrain of modern politics by knowing the fundamental forces behind these changes and their possible consequences. Societies may exploit the transformative potential of power transitions to create more robust, equitable, and democratic political systems by practicing inclusive governance and strategic foresight.

6: Reactions and Controversies

The mapping of legislative boundaries is a highly consequential process. It draws the lines that define the fluctuations of political power and form the basic framework of representation. But this process has frequently been tainted by disputes, with gerrymandering—the act of drawing boundaries in favor of one political party over another—casting a lengthy shadow over election legitimacy and fairness. Wisconsin's recent redistricting attempts provide a glimpse of light in the heartland of America, indicating a shift away from partisanship and toward a more representative form of governance.

State lawmakers' responses

State lawmakers responded fervently to the release of Wisconsin's new legislative maps, expressing the deeply ingrained interests and worries entwined with the redistricting process. The opposition lawmakers expressed doubt, accusing the ruling party of partisan bias in the boundary drawing, while supporters of the ruling party celebrated the maps as a victory of equitable representation. With a majority in the legislature, Republican lawmakers praised the maps for reflecting election realities and highlighting the importance of stable governance. Democratic politicians, on the other hand, objected, pointing to examples of packing and cracking—tactics designed to distort or concentrate a community's voting strength to alter the electoral balance.

Communal Response to the New Legislative Maps

The public's reaction to the new legislative maps echoed throughout communities outside of the state legislature's chambers, shedding light on the range of viewpoints and goals that are interwoven within democracy. Advocacy groups and grassroots organizations gathered to examine the maps and held public forums and town halls to increase support for fair and transparent redistricting. Driven by a feeling of civic responsibility, citizens examined the maps with an eye toward inclusivity and fairness, highlighting the significance of maintaining democratic values during the redistricting process. But despite the din of voices, doubt persisted, with some doubting the integrity of political promises to put the good of the public above party interests.

Concerns and Criticisms Voiced by Opponents

Critics of the new legislative maps in Wisconsin presented a long list of grievances and objections, pointing out alleged inconsistencies and unfairnesses in the redistricting process. Legal professionals and civil rights organizations criticized the maps, citing statistical irregularities and departures from accepted standards for equitable representation, as evidence of gerrymandering. Fears that their voting strength would be diminished were expressed by communities of color, highlighting the necessity of guaranteeing minority participation in the halls of power. In addition, watchdog organizations expressed concern about the lack of openness and public participation in the redistricting process and demanded increased responsibility and supervision to protect election integrity.

Assessing the Legitimacy and Fairness of the Redistricting Process: In the face of conflicting interests and ideologies, assessing the legitimacy and fairness of Wisconsin's redistricting process necessitates a careful analysis of institutional safeguards and democratic standards. Experts examine the extent to which boundaries represent communities of interest, political neutrality, and compactness by closely examining the criteria employed in map drawing. In addition, the use of technology in redistricting is questioned; while improvements in mapping software have made it possible to draw boundaries with better accuracy, they have also given rise to worries about algorithmic bias and manipulation. Beyond details, the redistricting process's impact on public confidence and involvement serves as a barometer of fairness, highlighting the necessity of openness, responsibility, and civic engagement in determining the boundaries of democracy.

Beyond Gerrymandering: The Prospect for a More Representative Government Awarded by Wisconsin's New Legislative Maps:

Amid divisive discussions and opposing viewpoints, Wisconsin's new legislative maps provide a glimmer of optimism for those who want a more representative government. Even while gerrymandering remains a real threat, the rise of grassroots action and legal challenges highlights how democratic institutions are resilient in maintaining the idea of one person, one vote. Furthermore, the growing public outcry and bipartisan alliances driving redistricting reform represent a paradigm shift toward inclusivity and fairness in the political process. The road beyond gerrymandering provides a tribute to democracy's enduring potential to transcend party boundaries and defend the collective will of the people as Wisconsin forges ahead toward a more egalitarian future.

Wisconsin's redistricting process is a microcosm of the country's larger fight for representative government. The nation is currently grappling with the legacy of gerrymandering and the loss of democratic norms. Wisconsin's history offers valuable lessons that extend well beyond its boundaries. We can create a more ideal union where all voices are heard and every vote matters by embracing accountability, openness, and civic involvement.

7: National and Broader Context

In the continuous fight for equitable representation in American politics, Wisconsin's recent revision of its legislative districts represents a critical turning point. The emergence of these new maps, while the state struggled with the complexities of gerrymandering, not only changes Wisconsin's political landscape but also provides important lessons for other states, sparks hope for future reform initiatives, and emphasizes the significant impact on democratic processes and representation. In this talk, we examine the complex effects of Wisconsin's new legislative maps, including their bearings on national politics, their lessons for other states, the prospects for gerrymandering reform initiatives, and their wider effects on representation and democratic processes.

Effect on Politics at the National Level

Wisconsin's new legislative maps have an impact on national politics that goes well beyond the state's boundaries. Wisconsin, a state with a long history of divisive gerrymandering lawsuits, is sending a strong statement to the rest of the country with its move toward more fair representation. These designs disrupt the prevalent narrative of political polarization and paralysis by tearing down entrenched partisan advantages and promoting competitive voting districts. Furthermore, they indicate an increasing need for responsibility and openness in the redistricting procedure, which is forcing other states to reevaluate their methods of creating electoral borders. Wisconsin gives new life to larger attempts to strengthen democratic institutions across the country as it establishes a precedent for more equitable representation.

Lessons for Other States

The state of Wisconsin's transition to a more representative democracy provides important lessons for other states facing gerrymandering issues. Fundamentally, the Wisconsin experience serves as a reminder of how crucial grassroots activism and public participation are to bringing about significant change. Wisconsinites organized to demand a more equitable redistricting process through coordinated advocacy activities, community engagement, and legal challenges, proving the effectiveness of group action in defending democratic values. Additionally, the establishment of independent redistricting commissions, as demonstrated in Wisconsin, offers a workable paradigm for guaranteeing increased transparency in the map-drawing process and reducing party influence. States around the country may take a cue from Wisconsin's experience and steer toward more inclusive and equitable representation for all citizens by embracing innovation and collaboration.

The Future of Reforms to Gerrymandering

The new legislative maps in Wisconsin are a driving force behind national gerrymandering reform initiatives. Calls for extensive change are gaining traction as the public grows more conscious of the negative consequences of party boundary manipulation. The effectiveness of nonpartisan methods in fostering justice and accountability in the redistricting process is demonstrated by the accomplishments of

Wisconsin's independent redistricting commission. Advocates and legislators need to take advantage of this momentum going forward and implement significant reforms that put the needs of voters before partisanship. A more democratic and representative political environment appears to be in store for the future of gerrymandering reform, if it embraces innovation, makes use of technology, and codifies concepts of justice and equity into legislation.

Impact on Representative Democracy and Procedures

The adoption of more representative legislative maps by Wisconsin has significant ramifications for representation and democratic processes. These maps open the door to a more accountable and responsive government by encouraging competitive election districts and lessening the impact of partisan gerrymandering. Because elected officials are held to higher standards of accountability when serving their constituents, citizens are empowered to have their views heard. Furthermore, the increased focus on geographic compactness and community coherence guarantees that districts better reflect the population's different interests and demographics. This strengthens the legitimacy of elected officials, boosting public confidence in the democratic process and restating the fundamental idea of governance of, by, and for the people.

An important step forward in the goal of representative governance has been taken by Wisconsin with the adoption of new legislative maps. The state leads by example by eliminating partisan gerrymandering and adopting fairness and equitable principles.

Wisconsin provides important lessons for other states facing comparable difficulties as it steers toward more participatory and transparent governance. Reforming gerrymandering appears to have a bright future as long as lawmakers and the general public continue to emphasize how important it is to protect democratic values. In the end, Wisconsin's story highlights democracy's ongoing endurance and the ability of citizens to work together to create a more ideal union.

Conclusion

In the continuous fight for fair and equitable representation in politics, **"Beyond Gerrymandering:** How Wisconsin's New Legislative Maps Provide Hope for a More Representative Government" represents a breakthrough. Wisconsin has been a national leader in election reform thanks to its careful research, calculated planning, and steadfast commitment to democratic values.

The release of Wisconsin's new legislative maps, which represent the result of significant efforts to counteract gerrymandering, represents a victory for accountability, openness, and inclusivity in the redistricting process. Through valuing community feedback, adhering to legal requirements, and utilizing technological innovations, decision-makers have established the foundation for a more thoughtful, equitable democracy that represents the needs of all constituents.

These new maps have far-reaching ramifications that go well beyond Wisconsin's boundaries. They are evidence of the effectiveness of judicial intervention, grassroots action, and bipartisan cooperation in the battle against partisan political boundary manipulation. Wisconsin can serve as a role model for other states facing comparable difficulties in navigating the complexities of redistricting fairly and ethically.

Furthermore, oppressed groups that have long been denied the right to vote due to gerrymandering's deceptive tactics have newfound hope after these new legislative maps are adopted. Wisconsin has made a significant step toward realizing the dream of a truly representative democracy, where every voice is heard and every vote counts, by encouraging greater diversity, inclusivity, and representation within the corridors of government.

But there is still a long way to go until a more ideal combination is reached. Even though Wisconsin has successfully implemented fairer legislative maps, we must continue to be on the lookout for attempts to subvert the democratic process in the future through partisan manipulation. Maintaining accountability of elected leaders and keeping fairness and equity at the center of our political processes will need sustained lobbying, monitoring, and involvement.

A moving reminder of the strength of democratic principles and the force of group action is provided by "Beyond Gerrymandering: How Wisconsin's New Legislative Maps Provide Hope for a More Representative Government." Let's renew our commitment to the continuous task of creating a more inclusive, fair, and just society as we commemorate this historic accomplishment. By working together, we can create a future in which every voter's voice is heard, every community is given more authority, and every election accurately represents the will of the electorate.